MAKING SENSE OF DREAMS

A Guide to Sleeping Better, Dreaming Better, and Understanding Your Dreams

Janette Marie Heart

For Stella

CONTENTS

INTRODUCTION

When was the last time you dreamt? What was it about? Was it in color? Were you a mere spectator or were you making decisions during the dream?

If you're like about 95% of people you won't remember what you dreamt of last night. And unless you're part of an even smaller percentage, you can't recall whether the dream was in color or black and white.

The reasons are manifold. One is you dismissed your dreams as silly and not worth remembering. Second your sleep was so bad you couldn't process your dreams properly. And third, you didn't bother keeping a regular record of your dreams.

This book will help try to help you remember and make sense of your dreams.

We divided this book into three major sections. The first section, What are Dreams? explores dreams as they appear in society. Here, we'll explore how dreams appeared in the Bible and other faiths. We will also briefly discuss the famous works of greats such as Sigmund Freud and Calvin Hall. We'll delve into how dreams have led to amazing discovering and breakthroughs and how dreams continue to have a profound effect on today's society.

In the second section, Give Your Dreams a Chance, we'll explore techniques on how to get a good night's sleep and increase the chances that you will dream. We'll also explore tactics we can use to better remember our dreams. One fascinating aspect about dream interpretation is that it's usually about context, hence the importance of recording several dreams, correlating them, and identifying patterns.

The last section, Common Dreams and Their Meanings forms the bulk of this book. It discusses common dreams, and the messages they may try to tell you. Together with techniques learned in the previous section, this will help you better understand what dreams are telling you.

Finally, a word of advise: It is best not to make life-changing decisions based on just one dream. Remember that context and patterns are essential when interpreting dreams.

If your dreams begin to affect your everyday waking life to the point that your mental and physical health has suffered, consider going to a therapist or physician.

WHAT ARE DREAMS?

In many cultures, dreams are ways of the divine to communicate with mortals. For some, dreams are symbols that need to be deciphered like a mystical message.

But for most of us, dreams are sequences of images, both moving and still, that appear to us as we sleep. These images affect as profoundly, triggering emotions and feelings. If the dream is lucid enough physical manifestation such as sweating or crying continue when we wake up.

Such is the power of dreams. And it's a power that we usually witness several times each night even if we hardly remember anything.

Dreams in the Bible
The Bible usually distinguished between dreams and visions. A person sees visions when she's wide awake, while dreams appear when the person is in a state of sleep.

There are 21 dreams recorded in the Bible and almost half, 10, came from its first Book—Genesis. And unlike in visions recorded elsewhere in the Book, they all appeared when the person was asleep.

The word dream also appears over one hundred times in the Bible. Though there are fewer dreams in the New Testament, they still usually serve the same purpose—the divine sending a message to the dreamer.

Among the most famous dreamers in the Bible were two

men named Joseph–Joseph also known as The Dreamer and St. Joseph, Mary's husband, and the legal father of Jesus.

Joseph the Dreamer was thrown to prison and interpreted the dreams of two inmates, both former officials of the Pharaoh. The cupbearer dreamed about serving the Pharaoh freshly squeezed juice. The chief baker dreamt of birds eating bread out of baskets intended for the Pharaoh. Joseph told the cupbearer that the dream meant that he'd be returning to his old post, while the baker was doomed for execution. Joseph's interpretation was correct.

Years later, the Pharaoh had a dream of seven skinny cows eating seven fat ones and seven withered ears of grain consuming seven fat ears. Joseph explained that there would be seven years of plenty and seven years of famine. Again he was correct, and the Pharaoh rewarded him with freedom and appointment as second-in-command.

St. Joseph had four dreams that had profound and lasting effects on Christianity. In two of these dreams, he received a warning to leave Bethlehem for Egypt, and then skipping Judea, and instead was told to go to Galilee. In another, he learned it was safe to return to Israel. And in a story familiar to Christians, while dreaming he learned of Mary's immaculate pregnancy, to let go of his fear, and to take Mary as his wife.

Dreams in Other Faiths

According to Buddhist legend, Maha Maya dreamed that a six-tusked white elephant descended from heaven, offered her a lotus, and entered her womb through the right side. This dream foreshadowed the future greatness of her son Gautama Buddha. Buddha would later achieve his awakening with the help of his dreams.

In other cultures, Morpheus is a god of dreams for the Romans and Greeks. The Vikings had Nótt, referred to by dwarves as dream-Njörun dream-goddess. The sacred script Quran also mentions dreams. Hindus also interpret dreams creations of Vishnu. Among the pleasant dreams in Hinduism is seeing Bal Krishna. It means there is prosperity in the house.

WHY DO WE DREAM?

Why do we dream? Why not just get a good night's rest, preferably eight hours or so and wake up refreshed? Why do dreams appear in our sleep?

One explanation is the REM sleep phase. In this phase, our brainwaves are almost as active as when we're wide awake. It is during this deep sleep that most vivid dreams occur. During this time, you may process thoughts from your awake stage. This may explain why pressing concerns usually find their way into our dreams, snipping at your thoughts and consciousness.

As with many things that people do involuntarily, dreaming helps us adapt and survive. This is the threat-simulation theory, which suggests that dreaming prepares us for threats in real-life situations, like in a rehearsal of flight or fight scenarios. Crafted by Finnish cognitive neuroscientist Antti Revonsuo, the theory claims that much or all of dreaming is "specialized in the simulation of threatening events."

This may explain why most people easily remember dreams about negative experiences or situation than friendly encounters. Negative experiences in dreams include arguments, walking in an unsafe neighborhood, living in a toxic work or home environment, etc. This triggers our fight-or-flight instincts as we deal with perceived threats, which friendly encounters do not.

Another study suggests dreams help us process what we're going through in our awake state. This explains why people who struggle with a problem suddenly find a solution after sleeping.

One difficulty in the academic study of dreams is the lack

of data. Researchers usually depend on the subject's memory and self-reporting. Unfortunately, this also means that the subject has forgotten others, which would give a complete and better picture.

Hall

Calvin Hall, an American psychologist advanced his cognitive theory of dreams. This states that "dreams express 'conceptions' of self, family members, friends, and social environment. They reveal such conceptions as 'weak,' 'assertive,' 'unloved,' 'domineering,' and 'hostile'. In other words, "dreams reflect the dreamer's unconscious self-conception which often does not at all resemble our trumped up and distorted self-portraits' by which we fool ourselves in waking life; dreams mirror the self."

For example, if one dreams of being attacked by a current lover, even if there is zero hint or sign of the propensity to be violent, this may be driven by a fear of relationships, either driven by fear of loss or inadequacy. This may have nothing to do with that person, but by our perceptions.

In his theory on the concept of others, Hall believed dreams are suggestions of our biases. If a person is nice, he would most likely be nice in your dream. If he is mean, that person may also be mean in your dreams.

Freud

In 1899, Sigmund Freud, the founder of psychoanalysis, published his seminal work The Interpretation of Dreams. In that book, he introduced his theory of the unconscious and how it relates to dream interpretation. He believed dreams are products of one's psyche.

In Freud's view, all dreams are forms of "wish fulfillment," or the satisfaction of desire through an involuntary thought process. He believed dreams were puzzles, but when interpreted properly form a "poetical phrase of the greatest beauty and significance."

THE POWER OF DREAMS

Dreams are powerful. And as we shall see in the next sections, the have had a profound in religion and history.

DREAMING BIG

Psychologists have long suggested that our dreams affect our daily lives. Dreams and goals usually provide hope and a blueprint on how to proceed. These give people purpose. In contrast, people who don't dream big or to even improve their situation end up feeling empty and hopeless.

For some people, dreaming big always mean a brighter future with two components. First is a fantastic dream where you become famous, rich, etc. If you're a musician, you're probably dreaming of topping the Billboard charts with every release. If you're a computer programmer, you're probably dreaming of the next TikTok or Google or Facebook.

The second item means improving their current situation. It can mean quitting a job you hate and doing what you really want, even if the pay is smaller. Dreaming about it helps you plan and mitigate the risks of such a move. These increments may not always lead to achieving the fantastic dream, but will definitely improve the person's outlook and chances for success.

As a person continues of dreaming of a brighter future, this carries over when she's asleep as if the subconscious is trying to refine and process your "awake" dreams and thoughts.

The giant goal and the smaller goal eventually lead to a more fulfilled individual.

BREAKTHROUGHS AND IDEAS THAT APPEARED IN DREAMS

Theory of Relativity

Probably the most famous dream that resulted in a scientific breakthrough was the one Albert Einstein had. In his dream, he was walking through a farm surrounded by an electric fence. When the farmer turned the fence off, he and Einstein witnessed the same thing, but saw the events differently. Einstein saw the cows jump at the same time, while the farmer saw them jump one by one like in a Mexican wave.

In another dream, Einstein was sledging along the mountain when he noticed the stars changed their appearance as he traveled.

These inspired Einstein's Theory of Relativity as he woke up realizing that events could vary from different perspectives.

Google

Google's co-founder Larry Page dreamt he could download the entire web to a computer. When he woke up in the middle of the night, he began creating what would eventually become Google.

DNA

DNA was already known in 1869, mainly because of Swiss physician Friedrich Miescher, but it was only in 1953 when the familiar double helix structure was discovered. Dr. James Watson dreamed of a spiral staircase and two intertwined snakes, paving the way for the image now familiar to even non-scientists.

Sewing Machine

Elias Howe had been struggling to perfect his sewing machine, and his breakthrough came in a dream. He dreamt cannibals were stabbing him with spears that had a hole in the tip. He realized that the needle in his machine needed a hole in the tip instead of the other end.

The Periodic Table

Russian chemist Dmitri Mendeleev had spent a decade trying to organize the chemical elements in a sensible pattern. After an exhausting day, he fell asleep and dreamt of a table where everything fell into place. The result—the periodic table familiar to all students of Chemistry.

Analytic Geometry

In 1619, German mathematician and philosopher René Descartes had a series of dreams where he questioned the nature of reality. Among the results from his dream was the invention of Analytical Geometry where he linked the previously unrelated topics of Algebra and Geometry.

Yesterday

The melody for the Beatles' classic, Yesterday came to Paul McCartney in a dream. As he couldn't think of the words immediately, he had lyrics about scrambled eggs. He thought he had heard the melody before, but when he asked around and nobody was familiar with it, he knew the tune from his dream was original.

Later in his career, a dream about his deceased mother inspired another classic. Amidst rising tensions in the band, Paul's mother Mary appeared and consoled him. The result was the song, Let It Be.

Satisfaction

Inspirations that came while asleep weren't exclusive to the Beatles. Keith Richards, the lead guitarist of their contemporary and rival, The Rolling Stones, came out with a classic riff in a dream.

He went to bed with his guitar and the tape recorder on. In between the snoring, there was a riff that would introduce the classic song, Satisfaction.

DIFFERENT TYPES OF DREAMS

Depending on which psychologist or study, there are several types of dreams. Freud named two main types, while others have identified nine. Here are the most common types of dreams.

Daydreams

Daydreams are dreams people have when they're physically awake and usually doing their regular daily tasks. At school, a student may dream of a crush. At work, an employee may daydream about his date later that night. Though physically awake, the daydreamer usually becomes detached from his physical environment, with his attention focused on what he's daydreaming about. In movies, this is usually depicted as the daydreamer being rudely awakened by a person of authority.

Sometimes, while daydreaming the physical actions and the dream are almost one. For example, a girl daydreams about her crush even as she continues to doodle his name on her notebook.

Nightmares

Nightmares are disturbing and scary or fear inducing dreams. Sometimes these are so powerful that the dreamer wakes up, often shaking and sweating, and screaming. Stressors from the dreamer's usual awake state usually cause nightmares, and likely invade his thoughts during daytime. Recurring nightmares are usually signs of trauma or extreme stress.

Nightmares are common with soldiers who have traumatic

experiences, and diagnosed with Post Traumatic Disorder Syndrome (PTSD). In some tragic cases, they take their own lives, as they can no longer cope with nightmares and the pain they feel.

False-Awakening dream

In this kind of dream, the dreamers believe they are already awake. In reality, though, they remain in the middle of a dream.

Night terrors

Children usually experience night terrors. They wake up shaken and usually afraid, but sometimes rarely remember what they dreamt about.

Lucid dreams

Lucid dreams are dreams where the dreamer is not just like a movie viewer, watching events unfold. Instead, she can control her actions and thoughts during the dream itself.

Prophetic Dreams

We usually attribute prophetic dreams to a divine being with a message about a future event. Most recordings of dreams in the ancient world, from the Babylonians to the Sumerians, are about this. In some cultures they have a sacred site, which pilgrims visit such as a temple or shrine. Here they prepare themselves in rituals before seeking help from a divine being, usually in a dream.

In the Netflix series about the Vikings, the protagonist went to the temple at Uppsala where she met a spirit guide who gave her a glimpse of her past and a cryptic warning about moving forward.

GIVE YOUR DREAMS
A CHANCE

HOW TO SLEEP BETTER

The primary key to having and remembering dreams is to sleep deeply and better. You can't dream if you're spending hours on your bed tossing and turning and staring at the ceiling.

Here are ways to get better sleep.

Regular Sleep Schedule.
Aim to have a regular sleeping and waking up time, even on weekends. This will train your body to seek sleep at particular hours of the evening as your habit reinforces your body's sleep-wake cycle.

A key is to have a bedtime routine. For example, you brush your teeth, put on your pajamas, and turn off the lights, etc. in sequence. This routine will tell your body it's bedtime.

Pay attention to your circadian rhythm

Your body has a natural sleep-wake cycle known as your circadian rhythm. This is a 24-hour cycle that is part of your body's internal clock. If this clock is off or malfunctioning, your body won't get the necessary prompts to sleep. This may cause lack of sleep and may lead to insomnia.

Jet lags usually disrupt your circadian rhythm. Travelling to different time zones, especially ones with at least a six-hour difference can wreak havoc on your sleeping patterns, and your body will take a while to adjust. Among the ways to deal with this is to get as much sun exposure as possible. Natural sunlight or bright light during the day keeps your circadian rhythm working.

Watch what you eat and drink

Avoid going to bed starving or full, as either will disrupt your body's need to sleep. With a full stomach, it may be true that you'll fall asleep faster, but sleep will not be as restorative as your body processes the food you just consumed. You're unlikely to reach the REM sleep phase.

You should also watch your caffeine consumption. For most people, drinking coffee past a certain hour will mean the inability to sleep. Some people, though, need coffee to fall asleep.

Watch your naps.

Napping may be healthy, but for some people, long naps may whack the body's internal clock. This differs per person and culture, though. For example, siestas are common in Spain, but there is no general insomnia crisis in the country.

It's best to listen to your body. When in doubt, keep your naps to about half an hour. This short power naps usually give the body the boost it needs, but not enough to disrupt your normal sleep later.

Exercise

People who exercise regularly during the day sleep better at night. Even light exercise such as walking can do wonders as blood flows better and the person's mood usually improves.

However, avoid exercising about three hours before bedtime. Your body needs to settle down and be relaxed before you go to sleep.

Take a melatonin supplement

Melatonin is the hormone that tells your body that it's time to sleep. It is a natural product found in plants and animals and has long been associated with the sleep-wake cycle.

Supplements ensure that you have enough melatonin

inside your body. This is particularly helpful when your travel to a different time zone as the supplement helps your body's circadian rhythm.

Prepare your sleeping environment.
Invest in a good bed, mattress, pillow, and blanket. These tools of sleeping will help you sleep better.

It is also best to keep your room cool. Aim for 20 degrees C or 68 degrees F—the temperature best for sleeping. Another area of improvement is keeping your bedroom dark.

Avoid electronics and social media before bedtime
The content that you consume might cause you anxiety and stressed, and will keep you awake. For example, a hurtful or angry comment on your social media post might unsettle or anger you, making sleep difficult.

The light from your screen also inhibits the production of melatonin.

Avoid alcohol
Alcohol may make you sleepy at first as it induces relaxation and sleepiness, but it the end it negatively affects your sleep and hormones. It will also disrupt your circadian rhythm.

This is the reason people who drink alcohol the night before feel groggy or grumpy upon waking up. And if you had a nasty hangover, it's unlikely you'll remember your dream.

Don't take liquids about two hours before bedtime.
A person who consumes a prodigious amount of liquids before bed, even if it's just water will probably suffer from sleep quality. This is because he will probably wake up in the middle of the night to relieve himself, because of nocturia or simply the need to urinate.

Empty your bladders before you go to bed
Aside from avoiding Urinary Tract Infections, emptying

your bladders before going to bed ensures better sleep. If your bladder is full, you will probably wake up in the middle of the night, right around the time when sleep is most restorative. This will disrupt your sleeping patterns or worse, you won't be able to go back to sleep.

There are psychologists who suggest drinking water just so the dreamer can wake up around the REM phase. This may work for a few, but for others, this disruption and inability to return to sleep can be stressful and counter-productive. Best to empty your bladders before bedtime.

Meditate
Few activities can quiet and calm the mind as meditation. This can be achieved with different techniques. A common technique is to imagine a tranquil place and slowly calm each part of the body until you drift to sleep. Others chant a mantra or repeat prayers until they fall asleep.

REMEMBERING YOUR DREAMS

Sleep well.
The first key ingredient in remembering your dream is to sleep well and at roughly the same time every night. This makes sure that your circadian rhythm is in sync with your body. It also ensures that you won't be fidgeting on your bed as you wait for sleep to visit you.

Decide to Remember Your Dream
Make a conscious decision to remember your dream. It may be just a simple reminder to your brain. Or you can use a mantra. Some psychologists suggest repeating a mantra like "I will remember my dream when I wake up." For some people, this is the final act before falling asleep, and has a profound effect on dream recall.

Wake up Rested
If your sleep patterns are working well, waking up will also come easy even without an alarm. Try not to open your eyes immediately upon waking up and enjoy your half-wake state. Stay in bed and let your mind drift for a few seconds before focusing on what you just dreamt about. Replay the dream in your mind. Note a few details like was it in color? Ask yourself how you felt after dreaming.

With practice, this dream recall sequence will come naturally. And since you're less likely to wake up grumpy, there is a greater chance that you'll remember your dreams.

Record your dreams

Grab your pen and journal once you open your eyes each morning and write whatever details that you can remember. Remember that your notes from the previous days might trigger something in your memory so it's important to record even trivial details. For example, you might remember seeing a strawberry in your dream the night before. And at that time it may seem out of place. But when recording a subsequent dream, you might realize that the strawberry was more significant than you earlier thought.

Alter your routine during the day

Changes in your regular routines may trigger new dreams. This may include taking public transportation instead of bringing your car. Or ordering coffee from another cafe. The experience will expose you to different stimuli that may help in creating dreams later.

Remember that the key to regularly remembering dreams is the same as with any habit. One must find what works with you and stick to it. Be consistent.

COMMON DREAMS AND THEIR MEANING

This section lists common dreams and their meanings.

BEING A DETECTIVE

Your gut feelings have probably been active and you think there is disloyalty or deceit nearby.

This dream generally means that the dreamer has recently been more suspicious, trying to find clues about problems around him or her. These problems may include a partner suspected of cheating, fraud, dishonesty, or disloyalty.

If you dream about being pursued by a detective, it may mean that one of your secrets from the past is about to haunt you and someone has been asking questions behind your back.

BEING A KING OR QUEEN AND SITTING ON A THRONE

Dreams about royalty are usually positive and may mean either of two things. It may mean you believe you deserve better and will get what you want or you are currently on top of the world.

It can also mean that you are ready to take on leadership roles and be responsible for others. This also means you are ready to make tough decisions.

Finally, it may mean abundance and glamour.

BEING ARRESTED

This dream is about loss of control.

This generally symbolizes losing control over some facet of your life or situation. It may also mean your stubborn refusal to act or fight for control.

For example, you have a bad habit that threatens to destroy your life and tear your family apart. In this case, this means that you probably need intervention to salvage the situation. Being arrested in your dream represents this intervention.

If your dream involves helping police officers arrest someone, it may be a good sign as you're probably helping that person correct his ways.

BEING A SUPERHERO

If you're successful or about to be, this dream usually means you've grown confident with your abilities and are not shy about letting the world know about it.

If you're struggling with school or work, it may mean a reminder that you can still overcome your troubles. This is especially so if the superhero is someone who transforms from someone weak to a powerful hero, like the boy who became SHAZAM.

BEING CHASED

Dreams about being chased generally means the dreamer is anxious and there's heightened stress about a forthcoming event, like a wedding, an important presentation, or performance, etc.

It is easier to understand this dream if you can identify the pursuer.

If the one chasing is a stranger, it may mean that the dreamer knows that there is a threat, but cannot understand or identify its source.

If the one chasing is a dog, it may mean that there is someone in your life that is mean, rude, or harmful. If the dog catches up and bites you, it may mean disloyalty and betrayal.

If the chaser is a cat, it may mean a fear of losing someone or something. This is common when the dreamer is going through personal issues with someone close.

If the cat bites you, it may mean someone close will let you down and exploit your vulnerability. If you end up fighting with the cat, it is also important to note the winner—is it the cat or you?

If an ex-lover is chasing you, even one you haven't seen in years, this probably means you should take your time before getting in a new relationship. It is possible that you still have issues that have to be resolved to give the next one a better chance.

Experts say that it is important to note that the dream is not always about your ex, it's about you. But it's different when you get intimate with him or her in your dream. (*See section on sex with your ex.*)

If the police are chasing you, it means you're running away from a person of authority or influence. The police represent authority, control, and power. You probably resent this person's influence, as you want to continue your reckless behavior. If you end up escaping from the pursuer, it may mean that you're willing to disappoint him or her and do what you want.

If a familiar member of the opposite sex is chasing you and you felt fear, it may mean that you are afraid of love. It may also mean that you are still healing from a previous relationship.

BEING IN A CAR

The meaning of dreams where you're inside your car depends on who the driver is. If you're the one driving, it probably means you're in control of your life, for better or for worse. If you're a grumpy passenger, it may mean that you don't like what's happening and intend to be vocal about it. If the car doesn't move, it may signify that your life's situation remains static—not going to be worse, and not going to be better.

The car's cleanliness is also a factor. If you have trash while driving, it may mean that you have a lot of baggage that you need to unload so you can travel more comfortably.

BEING LATE

Tardiness in dreams generally means struggling with expectations or changes.

It may mean that the dreamer is anxious about other's expectations. The dreamers may feel that they're unable to live up to a standard, either by his own or his environment. Tardiness means inability to meet an expectation.

BEING LOST AT SEA

In real life, being lost at sea means drifting aimlessly and being hopeless. Dreams reflect this meaning.

This dream may mean the absence or goals or direction in your life. It may mean that you're just waiting for things to happen, with neither willingness nor the ability to dictate what happens in your life.

You're trying to be hopeful, but you are afraid.

BEING NAKED

Dreams about being naked in public usually means vulnerability and fear people will find this weak spot.

This may also mean that the dreamer thinks she's a fake and if found out would be subject to ridicule.

For example, the dreamer may be a successful person who has a deep secret that could undermine everything she built. The same with people who always put up a brave front and being strong for others. They may have a hidden fear that people will realize that they, too, are struggling in some form within.

(*Also check out Nudity or Being Dressed Inappropriately in Public*)

BEING YOUNG AGAIN

Dreams about a return to your youthful days usually mean a feeling of inadequacy or suffering from neglect. When you were young, you probably got a lot of attention, but now that you're older, you don't get as much even from your partner.

If may also mean that as you got older, you could no longer do the things you did when younger.

BURIED ALIVE

This dream means that you are being suffocated by a current situation and you're struggling to find a way out.

You are desperate about something and time is running out.

CHANGING THE COLOR OF HAIR

Just like in real life, dreams about changingyour hair color signify a major change in your life.

Dying your hair in your dreams from white or grey to black may mean a hidden and unfulfilled desire to recapture your youth. Dyeing it black may also reveal depression or no longer finding joy in anything.

Vibrant colors such as yellow, orange, or blue, etc. may mean that you're fulfilling the desires of your inner child. You're probably smiling as you look at the mirror.

CHASING SOMEONE

This dream usually means you are attracted to someone.

The distance between you and the one your chasing represents your chances of success. If the distance is insurmountable, it probably means you have no chance or you need a different approach. If the person is within reach, it may mean that the person will reciprocate your feelings.

Just note the person's reaction when you finally catch up with him or her. Joy signifies the feeling is mutual. Disgust means otherwise.

DISCOVERING A NEW OR SECRET ROOM IN YOUR HOUSE

This generally means several things. First, you are discovering things about yourself that you didn't previously know about. For example, a talent in music or sports just revealed itself. It can also mean that your gut is telling you that despite your limiting beliefs, you can still improve on something, for example at school or work.

The second meaning is that someone is keeping a secret from you. It can be deliberate or probably the person didn't think you needed to know.

If you discover many hidden rooms at the same time it may also mean that you're about to come across great wealth or great improvement in your life.

DROWNING

If you dream about drowning it probably means you're being overwhelmed by a current situation and you're struggling to stay afloat. This is especially true if you're calling for help in your dream, someone sees you, but ignores you. It may mean that you're on your own.

If you're drowning someone in your dream, it may mean that you are suppressing emotions, usually rage and resentment, towards that person.

DYING

Another dream that leaves the dreamer upset or disconcerted is dying. This may involve the dreamer's death or of someone they know.

One interpretation is the "old you" is dying and a "new you" is being born. You may be going through a major transformation in your life. Your subconscious may be telling you that you're letting go of old things that no longer serve you well, and are making room for new ones. This may happen if there's a major change in your life, like a new job, city, or relationship. Or it may simply mean you have an epiphany on what matters most in your life.

Another interpretation is that you need to take charge of your life, that a part of you has to die to enable you to grow.

The manner of death is also important. A peaceful death may mean that you're welcoming changes in your life. A violent death may show otherwise.

But it's not always the dreamer who dies in the dream.

If you dream of a loved one dying, it may be a sign that you need to put an issue with that person to rest. Do you have unsettled issues with that person? Do you feel guilty that you don't spend as much time as you should with him or her? Do you refuse to admit the importance of that person in your life? Dreaming about that person's death may be a wake-up call.

If you dream of a graveyard with no funeral, it may mean that something from your past that has to remain buried has been dug up. Especially if the tomb is empty. If this secret from the past remains unexposed, it may be a sign that you are still consumed by fear of that exposure.

If your child dies in your dream, this may mean a fear that time has been passing by so quickly that the child will soon morph into an adult, and you will no longer be the center of his or her life. This may happen during an important milestone like walking for the first time, first day of kindergarten, first Holy Communion for Catholics, etc. The dreamer probably feels that the child will soon be an adult, have her own life, and move out.

For others, dreams about a recently deceased loved one may also indicate a message from the other side, a reminder to move on, as the deceased wants to be remembered but also to rest in peace.

Dreams about death are usually gentle reminders of how much (or how little) you've grown, how you need more time for the people in your life, and an opportunity for introspection to be more appreciative of the people and things surrounding you.

DOLPHINS OR WHALES

Dreams about dolphins and whales usually mean a willingness to listen to your subconscious or explore your spirituality. These dreams are usually inspirational, positive, and try to encourage the dreamer. As whales and dolphins are among the smartest mammals, they also symbolize awareness, intelligence, and instinctive gut feels.

If the dreamer is riding a dolphin, this usually means the dreamer wishes to advance in life.

If is also important to note where these wonderful animals appeared in your dream. If they're on land and outside their natural habitat, it may mean you're feeling out of place and are full of uncertainty. This means you should explore other areas of growth.

If you're trying to save these animals, it may mean you're trying to save a relationship or trying to preserve an old way of life that you cherish.

EATING GLASS

Dreams about eating glass can be jarring.

This disturbing dream signifies anger that's beginning to consume you. It can also signify frustration with something you've been doing with little or no success. For example, you're studying diligently yet your grades remain low. Or maybe you're working out regularly and watching what you eat, but you remain overweight.

The glass is usually a symbol of struggle that is consuming you.

EATING ICE CREAM

This means you are happy with your current situation and likely have a strong and supportive family.

FALLING

Dreams about falling usually mean a loss of control.

When a person falls from a great height, such as a flying airplane or a tall building, unless he has a parachute, he is in the mercy of gravity and loses control over his fate. The same is true with dreaming about falling—they usually mean a loss of control over something important to the dreamer.

It may mean the dreamer feels inadequate in certain areas of his life. It is usually a reflection of helplessness in a current anxiety, fear, or terror over a situation.

It may also mean that the dreamer, despite knowing it might be good for her, refuses to let go of something. This can be love, a job, or material things.

If the dream of falling persists and affects your awake state, you might need to see a physician.

FRUITS AND VEGETABLES

Fruits, vegetables, and other plants in dreams usually signify fertility and reproduction.

<u>Bananas</u>

Dreams about bananas usually mean happiness and good fortune. Happiness because bananas have tryptophan which improves your mood and makes you happier. Dreams about bananas imply good fortune because they come in bunches. Trees are also usually easy to plant and nurture.

As bananas are also phallic symbols, dreams about the fruit may have sexual meanings.

Depending on the dreamer's feelings during the dream, it may mean comfort in one's sexuality and meeting sexual needs or it can mean frustration. Depending on your lifestyle, bananas served with chocolate or ice cream in your dreams may mean a desire for sexual experimentation. Or it may have non-sexual meanings, but are just a manifestation of your desire to enhance everyday activities.

<u>Cabbages</u>

Dreams about greens in general mean a fresh start. Besides this, cabbages symbolize purity and fertility. This means that if a woman dreams of eating cabbages, she may ovulate and get pregnant soon.

<u>Celery</u>

Dreams about celery may signify an unexpected source of happiness. For example, it may come as being accepted in a job you applied for a long time ago and have given it up as lost. Or it can be reconnecting with someone from your past and you're now both available and open to a relationship.

Coconuts

Dreams about coconuts are usually positive. After all, coconuts arealled the fruit of life. Everything, from its trunks to its leaves, to its fruits and shell are useful. So it is no surprise that it means prosperity and flexibility.

It may also mean that you have all the parts needed to construct a solution to a problem that has been bothering you.

If you're dreaming of a tropical setting, of beaches lined with coconut trees, it may mean that you are either relaxed or need a break.

Grapes

Dreams about grapes usually signify the coming of more blessings and happiness in your life. They symbolize abundance and rewards for hard work.

Sometimes, this dream means unexpected wealth coming to your life, such as inheritance or winning the lottery.

Kale

Kale, like other leafy vegetables symbolize prosperity. However, it has the additional probable meaning of anxiety and a general bad mood.

Since kale is associated with many weight-loss diets, this may also symbolize the sacrifices you've been making to be healthier or other goals.

Lemons

Lemons along with other citrus fruits like oranges usually represent good luck. Lemons also represent abundance and health.

Sometimes, dreams about lemons mean that despite abundance, something, usually a relationship is about to turn sour. This may lead to a cleansing in your life.

Oranges

Dreams about oranges usually mean health, depending on the state of the fruits in your dreams. Fresh oranges mean good health. Rotting oranges mean health problems.

If someone gives you oranges, it may signify that he is planning to share his feelings. A proposal or marriage may be coming. If someone you're not close to gives you oranges in your dreams, it may mean that the person has a secret affection for you or you have a lingering disagreement with him that you need to resolve.

Papaya

Dreams about this have a lot to do with the fruit's state. If it's ripe, it usually means good fortune. If it's not, it means the opposite, or at least you have to wait a while before good fortune visits you. Rotten papaya may mean health problems.

Pear

Dreams about pears are generally positive, as ripe pears are symbols of fertility and prosperity. The dream could mean success and new opportunities. In some cultures, ripe pears are a symbol of reproduction and dreams may signify wedded bliss with healthy children and a comfortable family.

Pineapples

Dreams about pineapples usually mean good fortune, happiness, joy, and abundance. For the business owner, it may mean good profits from a transaction. It may mean marriage with a suitable partner for the bachelor or single woman. For married women, it may mean pregnancy.

However, as with other dreams about fruits, if they're rotten or unripe, either you have health problems or the blessings are still on the way.

Strawberries

Strawberries like bananas have sexual connotations when they appear in dreams. Women with a half-eaten strawberry on their lips usually signify seduction.

Eating strawberries in your dreams may mean that you are currently enjoying or about to enjoy a passionate and pleasurable sexual relationship.

Tomato

It means luck is coming to you in the next few days. It can be money or advancement in your career or a new and more exciting relationship.

Zucchini

Dreams about zucchinis usually tell you about your enthusiasm and energy.

It may also represent a healthy sexual appetite.

FINDING MONEY

Money in dreams symbolizes prosperity. So finding money in dreams means you recently or will soon find abundance. This is not limited to financial wealth. This abundance can mean happiness in your personal life, or improved health.

FLYING

Dreams about flying generally mean escaping from your current situation. It can be about people, relationships, career, etc. that impede your sense of freedom and satisfaction. It can also mean that you've broken free from society's norms and prefer to acknowledge whom you are. This may also refer to your sexuality and your willingness to accept who you are.

Flying in whatever situation usually means you are about to or have taken control of your situation. Since you are hovering above everything, you can see the bigger picture and can plan your next moves to improve your situation.

A negative meaning about flying in dreams is that there's a subconscious belief that you are better than everyone else and that you need no one's help. This may be linked to superheroes such as Superman who can fly and usually do the helping, not the other way around.

Note that this is different from falling where you have no control about what's happening.

HAVING A BABY

Dreaming about having a baby, regardless of your relationship status usually signal a major change. Just like having babies in real life means the parents or guardians need to change their lifestyle, you may have to do the same.

HAVING A PARTNER EVEN IF YOU'RE CURRENTLY SINGLE

It means that someone will probably come into your life and have a relationship with you.

Check your feelings from the dream. If you were happy then that person is a gift. If you were miserable in the dream, it may be wise to stay away from that person.

HAVING SEX

The meaning of sex in your dreams depends on who your partner is. While it is possible that you are sexually attracted to some participants in your dream, it doesn't mean that you're sexually attracted to all of them. Sometimes, it may only mean that you want to get closer to him or her.

For example, sex with a boss in your dream may mean that you only want to emulate him and pattern your career after his. If it's with a friend, you may be suppressing your desires for fear of losing the friendship.

Sometimes, sex with a stranger (unfamiliar, faceless, or wearing a mask) in your dreams doesn't even refer to sex. It may just mean that you have goals you haven't come to terms with.

If dreams of having sex with another person persist, it is best to discuss the situation with your partner or a professional.

HAIRCUT

Dreams about haircut imply changes in your life.

It can either be negative or positive. For example, dreams about someone cutting your hair without your permission may signify disloyalty or betrayal as in the story of Samson.

If you're the one who initiated the haircut in your dreams, it may mean that you seek change. It's letting go of the past (failed relationships or unpleasant experiences at work), or you know you're ready to see the "new you."

INFIDELITY

This dream is unsettling for people in relationships. It can cause doubts and paranoia if not interpreted properly.

In general, a partner's infidelity in your dreams means one or both of you are not getting what you need from your relationship. It may be attention, resources, sex, or simple appreciation. There may also be underlying and unresolved issues on trust and communication.

A key question to ask when having dreams like these is whether you're having enough satisfying sex. Sex at its most loving and purest is the best form of intimacy in a couple. If you're not and these dreams persist, communication with your partner or with the help of a therapist might help.

Another reason for this dream is a partner's previous infidelity. Have you moved on from this transgression? Is this something that you're willing to forgive and work around? Do you still trust your partner?

The person or thing that your partner cheated you with, in this dream is also important.

If it's with a stranger, it may mean something that is taking away time and attention in your relationship. This may be a new hobby or obsession. If it's with someone you know well, it may mean that that person has something that you want. A bigger house? More money? A baby, if you're childless and trying to conceive? Youth? It can be anything and it's usually something the other person has that you don't.

LOSING SOMETHING

When you dream about losing something and then searching for it, it may symbolize what you've lost or fear of losing. For example, if you're looking for your eyeglasses, it may mean that you no longer have the clarity of vision that you used to. If you're looking for a wallet, it may mean that money is a major issue. Or if you're looking for a wedding ring, it may mean that a relationship recently ended or is about to end.

LOSING TEETH

There are multiple meanings of dreams about losing one's teeth. Most of them mean dealing with a current or impending loss and changes, both imagined and real. This triggers stress or anxiety on the dreamers, which appear on their dreams.

Having your teeth fall out in a dream may mean dealing with the death of a loved one, the end of a relationship, losing your means of livelihood, etc.

If you dream of another person losing her teeth, it may indicate your negative sentiments about this person.

Growing teeth on the other hand may appear in children's dreams. It may mean fear of the changes in their bodies.

MASSIVE WAVES

This dream may mean being unprepared to handle a flurry of things that are coming at you. You may feel that you can't handle several things at the same time, overwhelming you like giant waves from the sea.

NUDITY OR BEING DRESSED INAPPROPRIATELY IN PUBLIC

There are variations in this dream. In the dream, the dreamer may be naked in public or wearing something inappropriate such as pajamas in the office. Or shorts in a black-tie event.

It usually means a feeling of being vulnerable or awkward. It may mean that you have revealed parts about you to someone or to the public that you should not have.

If you dream of being naked or being dressed inappropriately in a wedding, it may mean that you continue to seek someone's attention or love and everybody knows you should just give up.

It may also mean a fear that your secrets will be revealed to the world, leaving you vulnerable and naked.

OPENING A BAG

It usually means that change is forthcoming, and the excitement or dread is proportional to what you feel in your dream.

It may also mean that you're finally open to facing the unknown, not knowing what's inside the bag.

If you dream about suitcases, you may travel to a dream place soon.

If you dream of finding a bag on the street, its appearance and state are key to interpreting the dream. It is a good sign, though if the bag is in great shape, looks expensive, and full. If the bag is dirty, empty or with a suspicious smell, it may be a foreboding of something bad.

OPERA

Being in an opera may signify your presence in a formal setting and being surrounded by rich people. It may either mean enjoying it or there is intense discomfort. If it's the latter, and you find yourself in a similar situation in your working hours, your subconscious might be telling you to either adapt or to move to a different environment. For example, people with expensive or different lifestyles may surround you and there's a pressure for you to conform.

Dreaming about singing in an opera may mean a missed opportunity or a sign that you have to express your needs more forcefully and gain people's attention. Performing, whether singing or dancing in an opera may also mean that you're about to do something that will attract the attention of many people, something that may be an unintended result of your success.

Sleeping, especially snoring during an opera may mean that you're about to embarrass yourself in front of people who play a significant part in your life.

The meaning of dreams about operas extends to attending exclusive, snobbish parties.

PARALYSIS

This may mean that you're being stifled by your circumstances, probably because you're overthinking or have taken on too many tasks.

It may also simply mean that you think you can't escape your current predicament. Psychologists suggest identifying what that predicament is and improve your situation. Once you identify and resolve your issue, paralysis in dreams will probably disappear.

POOP

Ironically, poop usually means wealth when it appears in your dream. It is said that the bigger (and grosser) it is, the more fortune will come your way.

Stepping on poop means getting an unexpected fortune such as inheritance or a business deal that just came your way.

PREGNANCY

This dream may represent everything from new life to creativity to fear. It can also happen to anyone, regardless of one's feelings and aspirations about reproduction. Most times, it is not related to actual, biological pregnancy at all.

It can mean a new life or a new beginning for the dreamer. This is common for people undergoing major life changes like moving to a new city, a new job, divorce, or death of a person important to the dreamer.

If you are trying to conceive, it can be related to the stress or anxiety of being pregnant or a fear of inadequacy about being a good mother. A dream like this can also result from a recent lost pregnancy with the accompanying grief. Sometimes, women who have undergone abortion have these dreams as they process the terminated pregnancy and what their lives would be had given birth.

The pregnancy's term also reveals a clue to its meaning. If you're due soon, it may mean that a long-term project or goal is about to be completed. If you have more than one baby in your stomach, it may also mean that you have two or more items that you're currently doing and are trying to balance everything.

RETURNING TO COLLEGE

It may mean that you have a strong desire to increase your knowledge again.

It can also appear when you feel inadequate and this dream is a reminder that you've completed the rigors of college, that you can learn anything.

If however, your dream is about parties in college fraternity houses, it may mean that you're missing your youth when you felt freer to do what you wanted.

SEX WITH YOUR EX

This can be confusing, unsettling, and even embarrassing, especially if you've lost all feelings towards your former partner and are currently in a strong relationship. It can also mean that despite what you believe, you may not have healed completely.

What it means also depends on how you felt in your dream. If it's neutral or you felt nothing, it might simply mean nostalgia. If it was pleasurable, you're craving for intimacy with someone, and your ex was just a representation of what you desire. It is important to note that this dream does not necessarily mean that you want to sleep with your ex again.

If you felt meh and bored during and after the dream, it probably meant that you've changed, probably outgrown your ex, and the circumstances in your relationship.

SNAKES

Dreams about snakes may have contrasting meanings. On one hand, it may refer to a traitor or someone untrustworthy in your midst. On the other hand, it may also mean you're due for a renewal or major transformation as snakes shed their skins.

If you dream about being a powerful snake like a King Cobra, it probably means that leadership and prestige are coming your way.

SURGERY

If you recently had or are expecting a surgery or operation, there's a chance that you will have this dream. However, if you don't expect to be in a hospital soon, yet experience this dream, it may mean you need to remove something from your life. That something is not beneficial to you. It can be anything—a bad relationship, a bad habit, or bad mindset.

It can also mean that you're feeling something is wrong about your body, but you're too afraid to check with a doctor. Or you may feel that your doctors are missing something and they need to look harder.

The body part undergoing the surgery also provides clues on the dream's meaning. If it's the heart, you may need to check the health of your love life. If it's your head, you may need to rethink your mindset or change attitudes.

If you dream about someone else undergoing the surgery, it may mean you're worried about a loved one's health.

TAKING AN EXAM

Dreams about taking an exam usually reveal a fear of failure. Here it may be from a lack of preparation or a general feeling of inadequacy.

If you pass the exam, it means you have or can overcome the odds against you and succeed. If you failed, it means you need more faith in yourself and prepare better for challenges.

If you take the exam and something unexpected happens, like having questions on Spanish verbs in an English exam, you may be overthinking about your preparations and abilities in a coming exam or test.

TALKING TO THE PRESIDENT OR YOUR COUNTRY'S LEADER

If you dream about talking to the leader of your country, it probably means that you want to assume a position of leadership. This can be in both your professional and personal lives.

TALKING TO A DEAD PERSON

It generally depends on who the dead person is in your dreams. If it's someone close, it may mean that you have unsettled issues with him or her. It may also mean that you are undergoing a personal crisis and their presence, although only in this dreamy state, will bring you peace and comfort. In an earlier section, we discussed how Paul McCartney's mother appeared to him when he found himself in times of trouble, resulting in a song.

It may also mean that you are still processing their deaths and dreams appear to help you understand what happened and help you move on. These dreams tend to be more vivid as you go through the grieving process.

In some cases, there is a message from beyond, like revealing a hidden fortune or a plea for closure.

TALKING TO SOMEONE

When just before falling asleep, you think about a person or an event associated with that person, there's a chance that you'll dream of him or her. This is also true for people you may not have thought of for a while, but has a deep connection to your consciousness.

Context is always important, but in general it means there's an unsolved issue. You may need to know if the other person will reciprocate your feelings. Or maybe someone who harmed you or a friend with whom you had a falling out. Perhaps there was a rude server at the restaurant where you just had dinner and you wish you spoke your mind instead of just smiling. They can appear in your dreams.

They may also appear if we have powerful feelings and deep longing for that person. For example, our crush or someone we admire may appear in our dreams, probably because they dominate our daytime thoughts.

As with a lot of things that appear in our dreams, people can also be symbols of issues. The classmate who always beat you in Math contests when you were young may remind you how far you've gone and will probably be better than her in real life. The guy who rejected you may be a reminder that you avoided an unpleasant situation by not being with him.

Or if you are talking to someone who appears to be your child, and you're using your mom's words, you may be acknowledging that your mom's parenting was correct and plan to model yours with hers.

PLANE CRASH

Accidents whether via planes or other machines may mean that certain events in your life are out of control and you're just hoping for a miracle to save you and correct your course.

This helplessness may be a manifestation about your current situation where you're trapped.

UNABLE TO FIND A TOILET

This is a dream about one of the most uncomfortable situations a person might find himself in and is usually a symbol of anxiety and a stressful situation.

As using the toilet is a regular event for most people, not finding it in your dream may reveal a frustration with being unable to satisfy basic personal needs. It is possible that something that should come naturally or easily for you is not there.

It may also mean that time is running out on one of your endeavors.

If you find a dirty or unusable toilet, it may mean that you've been very helpful and people have been dumping their problems on you. This may also mean that all your helping has not been fully appreciated. The dream may be telling you to focus on yourself before helping others, similar to what they do in airplanes where the adult gets his oxygen first before helping a child or another person, lest they both perish.

Finally, there is the joke about having diarrhea and finding a toilet in your dream. Don't use it.

WEARING MISMATCHED SHOES

It means you have two divergent paths to choose from or conflicting feelings about a situation.

You have to make a major decision soon.

WEARING A RING

Rings are symbols of a union so it is possible that the dream is telling you that marriage or a civil union is coming soon.

If, however, you tried a ring in your dream, and it did not fit, it may mean that you are not ready or not interested to have a relationship with anyone.

WHITE DRESS

There are several meanings if you dream that you're wearing a white dress. This may be because the color white usually means perfection, purity, and hope. Stains and imperfections in the dress usually indicate a concern.

A white dress, especially a wedding dress, usually means purity. It may signify your positive growth as a person who others can plainly see.

It can also mean that you want to appear pure and innocent, even though you're not. This may be true if you're trying to hide the stains and damages in the dress.

If a currently married woman dreams of wearing a white wedding dress, it usually means an imminent pregnancy or a great desire to be a mother.

If you dream of a long white dress, it may mean that a surprise is coming. Something that you thought you would no longer be blessed with comes in your life.

If you dream of seeing, but not wearing a white, damaged dress, it may mean that your relationship has serious problems that need to be addressed. You and your partner may not see that, but the people around you do.

If you dream of trying on a white wedding dress, it may reveal a deep desire to be a bride, regardless of your age.

Dreams about someone wearing a white dress can mean several things. It may mean that you hold that someone in high regard. Or it can be visions of an ideal partner and you imagine him or her without flaws.

YOUR FAVORITE BAND THAT BROKE UP

If you are dreaming about a band that has broken up, and a member has since died, a dream about them may mean wanting a reunion that you know can never happen. This can be true with estranged or deceased close family or friends.

It may also simply be nostalgia about how different music or your lifestyle was years ago.

This can also be a symbolism for your desire to reunite with old friends, e.g. college and work but is impossible because of distance, death, or other circumstances.

YOUR OWN FUNERAL

Dreams about funerals usually mean closure and acceptance, more so if the funeral you're dreaming about is your own. There is finality in funerals and it appears in the dream's message. It may be asking you to find issues or situations where you need closure and acceptance.

Another meaning is the need to acknowledge a suppressed feeling or emotion. It may be trauma you chose to bury but never healed from or came to terms with. This denial may cause the dream, which suggests acknowledging it. This may cause either closure or resolution.

BOOKS BY THIS AUTHOR

The Dream Journal: My Dreams, Their Meanings, And Their Hidden Messages

The Dream Journal: My Dreams, Their Meanings, And Their Hidden Messages

Dreams communicate with us. The messages may come from our subconscious or something mystical and out of our ordinary world. Regardless of the source, dreams have messages. And we need to understand what is being said.

This journal will help you keep track of your dreams and maybe detect patterns and decipher hidden messages.

To help you in your dream journey, there is a short narrative on the meanings of common dreams.

So get this journal and start your journey. Great gift for your loved ones, too.

The Dream Journal For Single Women: A Notebook Of Aspirations And Contentment

If you're like most people, you remember dreaming, but hardly recall anything upon waking up.

Dreams are our bridge to the subconscious and the spiritual. They give hints on our fears, our aspirations, our insecurities, and our inspirations.

If you're single, you might dream about finding love and a happily ever after. Or you might dream about your career, your family, or your advocacies. But your dreams matter little if you can't remember them.

This journal can help you record your dreams, see patterns, and better understand what they're trying to tell you.

Special Features:

A guide on the most common dreams and their interpretations
An essay on how to answer the question: Why are you still single?

Great as a gift to single friends
This gift might change their lives.